Crocodiles

Written by Maggie Blake

A Survivor from Dinosaur Days

Crocodiles have lived on the earth
for millions of years.
They were cruising the waters
when dinosaurs roamed the earth.

Today, crocodiles live beside lakes
and rivers in Africa, Asia, Australia,
Central and South America,
and the southern tip of Florida
in the United States.
Sometimes they are found swimming
in the sea.

Crocodiles and Other Reptiles

Crocodiles are reptiles,
like lizards, snakes, and tortoises.
They have scaly skins and lay eggs.
When the weather is cold,
reptiles slow down.
They need the sun to keep them
warm and to give them energy.

At night, crocodiles like to stay
in the water, where it is warmer.
They crawl out at dawn to warm
themselves in the sun.

A Powerful Beast

Crocodiles are the most powerful
of all reptiles.
Some crocodiles grow up to
twenty feet long.

Crocodiles' skin is tough, like armor,
with spiky scales running down
their backs and their powerful tails.
They have sharp claws
and strong jaws for tearing
animals to pieces.

Crocodile Teeth

One of the most frightening things
about crocodiles is their teeth.
Crocodiles have lots of teeth,
hanging raggedly along their jaws.
These teeth fall out easily,
but new ones quickly grow back.
Each tooth can be replaced over
forty times in a crocodile's lifetime.

Did you know...?

You can tell the difference between an alligator and a crocodile by looking at their teeth.
A crocodile's fourth tooth sticks out on each side of its bottom jaw when its mouth is shut.
An alligator's fourth tooth doesn't stick out.

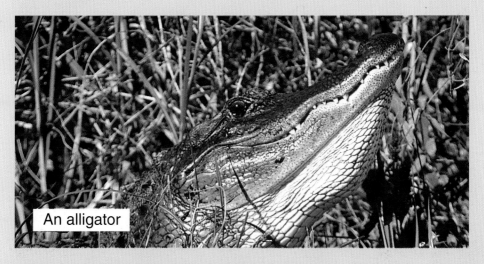

An alligator

A crocodile

Hunting

A crocodile often hunts at night.
It waits in the water with only
its nostrils and eyes above the surface.
When an animal comes too close,
the crocodile suddenly lunges sideways,
catching its prey in its jaws then
dragging it underwater to drown it.

Crocodiles can also crawl, trot, and glide quickly over mud and grass after their prey.

Crocodiles eat all kinds of animals. Some kinds of crocodiles eat mostly fish. Others eat anything they can catch, from large animals such as wildebeests or zebras to small birds.

Crocodiles cannot chew their food.
They tear off large bites,
which they swallow whole.

This crocodile in a wildlife park is being fed some meat, which it will swallow whole.

Territory and Nesting

Groups of crocodiles often
live together.
If a crocodile comes too close
to another crocodile's territory,
it may receive a swift bite on its tail.
Sometimes crocodiles fight
over their territory.

In spring, female crocodiles lay eggs.
They waddle out of the water to lay
about fifty leathery, white eggs
on the shoreline.
The nest is closed with a mixture
of mud, leaves, and grass
to keep the eggs warm.

Crocodile Babies

When they are ready to hatch,
the baby crocodiles tap their way
out of their shells.
They have a special egg tooth
to help them escape.

But the babies cannot burrow
out of the nest alone.
Their mother must dig them up.
Then she leads her babies
to the water or carries them gently
in her mouth.

For the next couple of weeks,
the mother crocodile stays
in or near the water with her babies,
while they learn to catch snails,
insects, and baby fish.

Many baby crocodiles do not survive.
They are often eaten by other animals
such as snakes, birds, turtles, and fish.
They may even be eaten
by bigger crocodiles.

A group of baby crocodiles

Crocodiles and Their Predators

Once a crocodile is fully grown, ,
it has very few enemies.
With its deadly jaws, not many
animals would dare to attack it.
Occasionally, however, a crocodile
has been killed by a lion
or a hippopotamus.

People are crocodiles' worst enemies. They have hunted and shot crocodiles, making their skins into handbags, shoes, and belts.

Saving the Crocodile

Today there are not so many crocodiles
left in the world.
Hunting crocodiles is now forbidden
in many countries, and many people
work hard to try to save
them from being killed.

These days many people believe
that crocodile skins look best
on crocodiles.

Index